OUR NEIGHBORS
IN AFRICA

John C. Caldwell
and
Elsie F. Caldwell

Illustrated by Heidi Ogawa

THE JOHN DAY COMPANY   New York

By John C. Caldwell

LET'S VISIT AMERICANS OVERSEAS
LET'S VISIT CEYLON
LET'S VISIT CHINA
LET'S VISIT FORMOSA
LET'S VISIT INDIA
LET'S VISIT INDONESIA
LET'S VISIT KOREA *with Elsie F. Caldwell*
LET'S VISIT MIDDLE AFRICA
LET'S VISIT THE MIDDLE EAST
LET'S VISIT PAKISTAN
LET'S VISIT THE PHILIPPINES
LET'S VISIT SOUTHEAST ASIA
LET'S VISIT WEST AFRICA
LET'S VISIT THE WEST INDIES

By John C. Caldwell and Elsie F. Caldwell

OUR NEIGHBORS IN AFRICA
OUR NEIGHBORS IN INDIA
OUR NEIGHBORS IN JAPAN

IN THIS BOOK YOU WILL READ ABOUT:

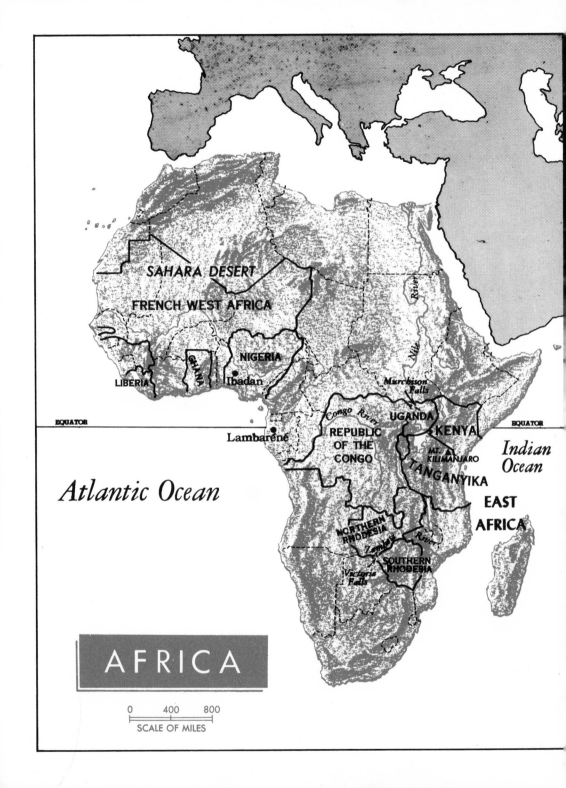

SAHARA DESERT

FRENCH WEST AFRICA

GHANA

NIGERIA

Ibadan

LIBERIA

EQUATOR

River

Nile

Murchison Falls

Congo River

UGANDA

KENYA

Lambaréné

REPUBLIC OF THE CONGO

MT. KILIMANJARO

TANGANYIKA

EQUATOR

Indian Ocean

Atlantic Ocean

EAST AFRICA

NORTHERN RHODESIA

Zambezi River

SOUTHERN RHODESIA

Victoria Falls

AFRICA

0   400   800

SCALE OF MILES

OUR NEIGHBORS
IN AFRICA

Our Neighbors in Africa

Have you seen movies or TV shows about Africa? Many wild animals live in the African jungles. In Africa there are lions and elephants, rhinoceroses and hippopotamuses.

The tallest people in the world live in one African country. These people are seven feet tall. In other countries there are pygmies who are only as tall as an eight- or ten-year-old American boy.

There are many interesting things about Africa. In some countries in Africa people wear no clothes. There are witch doctors who believe in magic. At the same time, Africans have built beautiful cities with high buildings.

Africa is not a country. It is a *continent*. A continent is much bigger than a country. The world has six continents, and Africa is the second largest. The United States is on the continent we call North America. There are three countries on our continent.

In Africa there are forty countries. Many different

people live in these countries. They speak more than five hundred different languages.

What Is It Like in Africa?

Do you see the picture of an African schoolboy? He has made a map of Africa, and is telling his father about the map.

This map can tell us interesting things about Africa. Near the top of the map the boy has written some D's. D stands for *desert*. In deserts little rain falls. It is so dry that few flowers or bushes or trees grow. In deserts much sand or rock is seen.

There are many places in Africa where there are deserts. One place named the Sahara Desert is the largest desert in the world.

In other parts of Africa there are thick *jungles*. A jungle is like a forest, but there are more trees and bushes and vines than in our forests. People who live in Africa call the jungle places *bush country*. All kinds of wild animals live in the bush country.

In the middle of Africa where the schoolboy is pointing there are high mountains. Some mountains are so

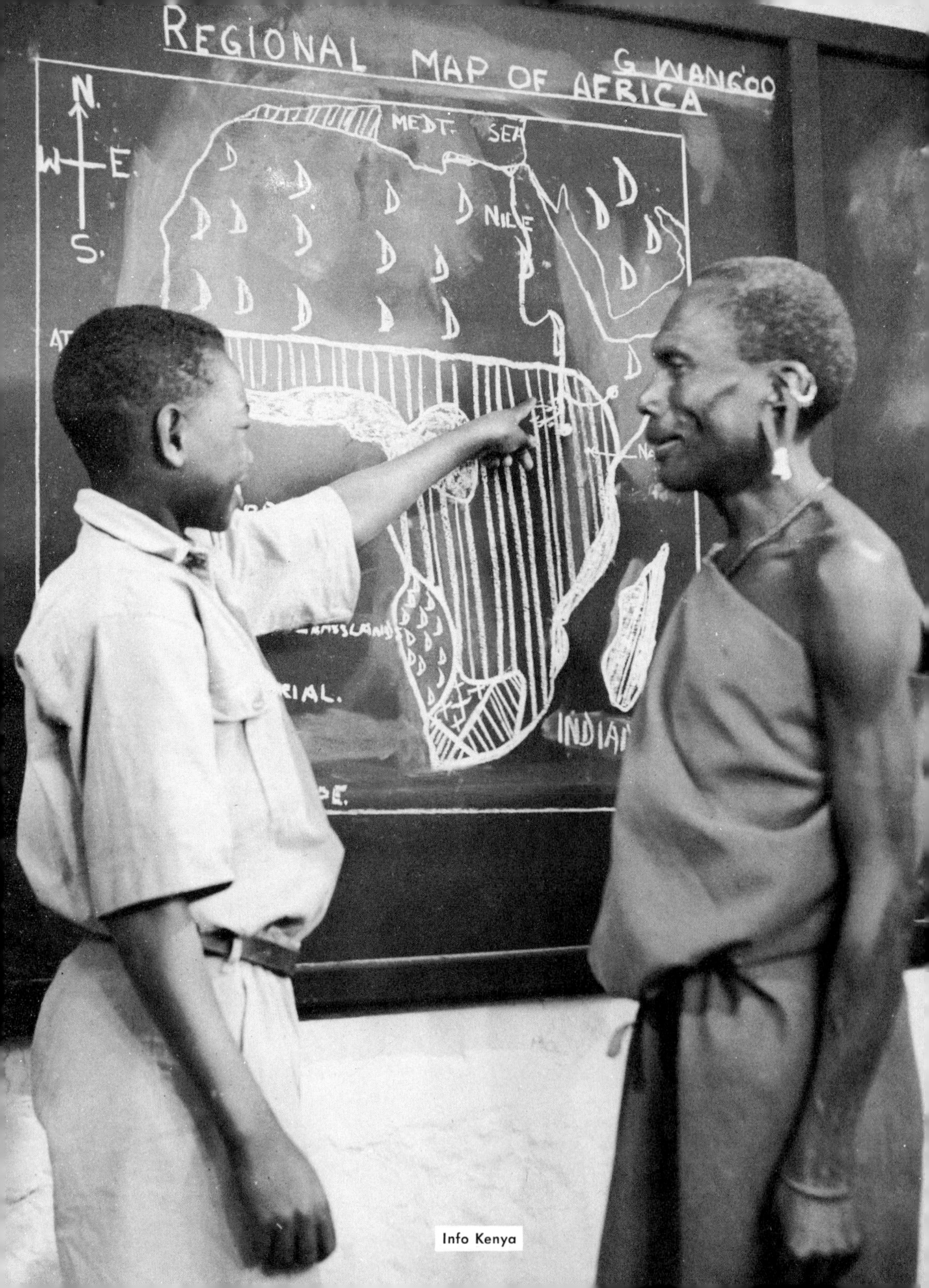

REGIONAL MAP OF AFRICA

G. WANG'OO

N.
W E
S.

MEDT. SEA

NILE

AT

RIAL.

GAMES LANDS

INDIAN

PE.

Info Kenya

Info Congo

high that even in summertime the tops are covered with snow.

In Africa there are big rivers and lakes. The second longest river in the world is in Africa. It is named the Nile. Another big river is called the Congo.

On this page you see a picture of the wide Congo River, with palm trees on one side and jungle on the other side. There are many crocodiles in this river.

Wouldn't it be fun to take a trip to Africa? Many Americans go there to hunt the animals that live in the bush. It is a beautiful continent.

We have learned that there are big deserts. The Sahara Desert is the biggest in the world.

The Nile River is the second longest in the world.

The mountains in the middle of Africa are covered with snow.

There are big lakes and waterfalls too. When I was in Africa, I visited Victoria Falls. It is on the Zambesi River (Zam-BEE-zee) and is one of the most beautiful waterfalls in the world.

The Weather in Africa

The equator is an imaginary line around the middle

Author

of the earth. In countries near the equator it is hot, and there is lots of rain.

The equator crosses the middle of Africa. The weather is hot, and sometimes it rains and rains and rains. The countries in the parts of Africa near the Atlantic Ocean and the Indian Ocean are always hot and wet.

The people who live in the middle of Africa have better weather. This is where high mountains are seen. In high places it is cool and pleasant.

In America we have fall and winter, spring and summer. In most parts of Africa the people know only two seasons. There is the rainy season when it may rain for days and days, and the dry season when the skies are clear.

Hot weather with much rain makes trees grow fast and tall. There are many palm trees in the hot parts of the world. If you lived in Africa you might climb a palm tree to get the coconuts.

In the deserts little rain falls, and the weather is very hot. Trees and flowers will not grow if there is no rain. But here and there in the desert there is a place called an *oasis* (oh-AY-sis). An oasis is a place where there is a spring of water or a well. The people who live in the desert build their houses near an oasis.

Here is another interesting thing about the Africans

who live in the desert: They ride on camels. Farmers in the desert use camels to pull plows.

Part of Africa is south of the line we call the equator. In parts of the world south of this line it is summertime when we are having our winter. And when we are having our summertime, it is the cool time of the year there.

In America, birds build their nests during spring and summer. But in many parts of Africa, the birds build their nests when it is fall or winter in our country.

Africa is an interesting continent. There are deserts where it is hot and dry. In the jungles or bush country, it is hot and wet.

In the middle of Africa, the weather is cool. There are

Info Congo

high mountains always covered with snow. The highest mountain is named Kilimanjaro. It is in a country called Tanganyika and is 19,340 feet high.

The People of Africa

We know there are forty countries in Africa. There are more than 500 different tribes.

Many Africans are Negroes, or Bantus, who are dark-skinned. Some Negroes and Bantus live in the northern part of Africa. There are also many people called Arabs who belong to the white branch of the human family.

In America we all speak the same language. If you live in California, you can talk to a boy or girl who lives in New York. But more than 500 languages are spoken in different parts of Africa.

Here are pictures of different Africans. The little girl belongs to a Bantu tribe in a country called Northern Rhodesia (Ro-DEE-sha). The language of her tribe is different from the language of the two women who are

Author

15

fixing their hair. They live in a country named Kenya (KEEN-yah).

The African woman carrying a big basket on her head lives in Southern Rhodesia. She does not speak the same language as the little girl or the other women.

Sometimes people living in one town cannot speak the language of people in the next village!

Houses in Africa

In the parts of Africa near the desert, houses are made of mud. The houses have flat roofs, and no windows. These houses look like little boxes.

Other African houses are small and may be round, or

Info Kenya

Info Rhodesia

they may be pointed like an Indian tepee. The walls are made of mud. The roof is made of straw.

There is one room in most houses. Very few Africans have running water, and most houses do not have a bathroom or a kitchen. When an African mother cooks, she may use a fire outside the house.

Many people do not have enough money to buy chairs and tables or beds. Many places in Africa have no electricity. African families often do not have electric lights or radios.

The small people we call *pygmies* make their homes by bending the branches of jungle bushes. They sleep under the branches.

17

Most pygmies live in a country named the Congo. They like to move from place to place. It is easy to make a house. So the pygmies often move from one part of the jungle to another.

Author

African Farmers

Do you like to eat candy bars? Chocolate is made from cocoa beans which grow on a small tree. Many cocoa trees grow in Nigeria.

On this page is a picture of two African girls picking coffee. Coffee beans also grow on trees. Farmers in East Africa grow tea and coffee.

African farmers raise cotton and corn, peanuts, and tobacco. In Africa, peanuts are called *groundnuts*, and corn is called *maize*.

Coconut palms grow in the hot, wet parts of Africa. Some of the coconut meat is dried and shredded and put

Info Kenya

in candy bars. More important is the oil which can be squeezed out of the white inside part of coconuts. The oil is used for making soap and for cooking.

Bananas also grow where the weather is hot and wet. In West Africa, there are many banana trees.

Food of an African Family

Do you think you would like banana soup?

Africans eat fresh bananas, fried bananas, roasted bananas, banana soup, and even porridge made with bananas.

Sometimes your mother may cook *tapioca* pudding.

Tapioca comes from the root of the *cassava* (ca-SAH-vah) plant, which is also food for many Africans.

There are cows in Africa, but most boys and girls do not drink milk because their parents do not know that drinking milk is important for good health. Very few people have enough money to buy fresh meat or vegetables.

Mealie meal is another important food. This is made of ground-up corn. Sometimes even babies are fed mealie mixed with water.

In Africa, corn meal is made by hand as in this picture. This is hard work.

Info Kenya

What Is a Witch Doctor?

When we are sick, we call a doctor. The doctor has many kinds of medicine to help make us well. Often when Africans are sick they call a *witch doctor*.

In the picture you can see what a witch doctor looks like. Witch doctors dress up in strange ways. The one in the picture has horns on his head. He is wearing beads. And on his back is the skin of a wild animal.

British Info Service

Witch doctors believe in magic. If someone is sick, the witch doctor dances, or says magic words to cure him. Sometimes he may make medicine from plants or parts of animals.

Because they have not gone to school, many Africans believe in magic and bad spirits and many gods. These

Info Kenya

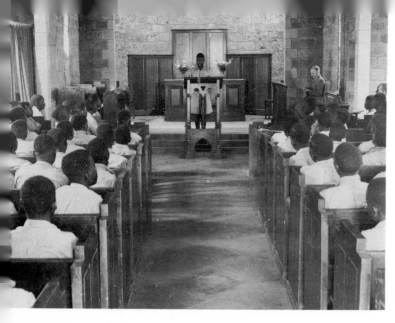

Info Kenya

people do not know about the medicine we use to cure sick people, so they call a witch doctor.

Africans like to dance. Often the witch doctor dances with the whole tribe. People put on strange-looking clothes. Several men sit on the ground beating drums.

In the desert parts of Africa, many people are *Moslems.* Moslems believe in God, and they call him *Allah.* Their Bible is called the *Koran,* and they worship in buildings called mosques (mosks).

There are many Christians in Africa. On this page you see a picture of African boys in Sunday school.

Many Americans have gone to Africa to be missionaries. They build churches and schools and hospitals.

How Africans Dress

In the hot parts of the world, people sometimes wear little clothing. Africa is a big continent, and people dress in many different ways. In the cities, there are people who dress just as we do in America. In the jungles, there are people who wear no clothes at all.

Many African women wear a dress made by wrapping cloth around and around their bodies. In the picture you can see the African women carrying things on their heads. In Africa, men and women, boys and girls too, carry heavy loads on their heads.

Each African tribe has a chief, as our Indian tribes do.

Author

The chiefs wear special clothes. On this page there is a picture of a chief. He is wearing a leopard skin and has a necklace made of wild-animal teeth.

The Big Cities of Africa

We have read about people who live in jungle villages and in the deserts. We have learned about people who wear strange clothes and about the witch doctors.

There are also big cities in Africa where people live as we live. There are tall buildings and wide streets. You can see that cars and trucks and buses are used in the cities.

Some African cities are very big. *Ibadan* (Ib-a-dan), a city in *Nigeria,* is the largest Negro city in the world. More than 500,000 people live there. Other big cities, too, are found in Africa. Some are beautiful, with very big buildings.

Going to School

There are big schools in the African cities. In the jungles, the schools are small. On the next pages are pictures of a jungle school and of boys and girls in a city school.

School children dress as we do. They study numbers

Info Rhodesia

and spelling and learn to read. Remember that many languages are spoken in Africa. Boys and girls study their own language. They also may learn English or French or Spanish.

At playtime African children like to play tag or hide-and-seek or singing games. And of course they like to play in mud.

Many African children do not go to school. There are

not enough schools or teachers or books. Many families do not have money to buy school clothes.

In Africa there are more children who cannot go to school than in any other part of the world.

Animals in Africa

On the next page you see a picture taken when I was in Africa. Can you read the sign? Wild elephants are

dangerous! There are places in Africa where it is not safe to get out of a car.

There are lions and elephants, hippos and rhinos in the bush country. Many kinds of monkeys are found in Africa. Animals called antelopes live here. In some places giraffes and zebras and wild buffaloes can be seen.

In a country called the Congo there are gorillas. Baboons are found in many places and are often very tame. One time we saw a baboon steal some cookies right off a table.

There are lions in Africa but no tigers. And did you

Author

30

Info Uganda

know that circus elephants come from India? African elephants are wild and hard to train.

What African animal do you think is most dangerous? Elephants are dangerous and so is the rhino. Gorillas are strong but are gentle animals unless people chase them. People in Africa believe the wild buffalo is the most dangerous of all the animals.

There are not as many animals in Africa now as in

years gone by. Many elephants have been killed by ivory hunters. The ivory tusks are worth a lot of money.

Many animals have been killed by hunters or because the animals damage crops. When big cities are built, animals are frightened and run away.

The countries in Africa do not want all the interesting animals killed. There are many places called game parks where no one may shoot the animals.

You may drive through a game park and see the animals from your car. It's fun to "shoot" them with a camera.

The Story of Slavery

Until Columbus found America, people from Europe did not know much about Africa. It was called the Dark Continent because so few white men had been there.

After the New World was discovered, Europeans began to travel to many faraway places. Ships began to visit West Africa. Many Europeans were ivory hunters. They killed elephants for the ivory tusks. Other Europeans began to capture Africans as slaves. Men and women, even boys and girls, were captured and taken far away to be slaves.

Many people became rich selling slaves. As many as 100,000 Africans were forced into slavery in a single year. Many Africans were taken to work in the American colonies, or to South America and the islands in the Caribbean Sea.

Because of slavery, we have many Negro citizens in America. Also because of the slave business, our country had a Civil War in 1861. There are many Negroes in South America and Central America and Cuba, also because of the slave trade.

The Europeans who began to explore Africa wanted ivory and slaves. They also wanted the minerals they found. On this page there is a picture of Africans working in a copper mine.

Info Rhodesia

European explorers found rich farmland in the high country where the weather is cool. And they began to cut the big trees that grow in the jungle.

Africans could not fight the European settlers and soldiers. They had big guns, but Africans used spears, or bows and arrows. Soon all of Africa was gobbled up by the European countries.

This is like the story of our pioneers and the Indians, isn't it?

Countries which belong to other countries are called *colonies*. We have a July Fourth holiday to remember when the thirteen colonies of America became free from the King of England.

It is because almost all of Africa belonged to other countries that African boys and girls study English and French, Spanish or Portuguese in school.

Now many African countries are becoming free, just as our people became free. Each year there are new countries in Africa.

The big cities with tall buildings were made by the Europeans who owned most of Africa. They built roads

and railroads too. They built big ships so that people could travel on the Nile River and the Congo River.

Some Countries in Africa

On this page we can see what the flags of some African countries look like. Remember that there are forty countries in Africa.

Let's learn the names of some of the African countries.

One of the biggest countries is called the Congo. It is in the hot part of Africa. The pygmies we have read about live in this country. The tall Watusi people who are often seven feet tall also live in the Congo.

The Congo belonged to Belgium for many years. It

Info Nigeria

is a rich country. There are copper mines and diamond mines too. Now the Congo is a free country. It is called the Republic of the Congo.

Another big country called Nigeria used to belong to England. It was an English colony, just as the thirteen colonies in America belonged to England.

On this page there is an interesting picture. The stacks that look like *pyramids* are made of bags of peanuts! Many peanuts are raised in Nigeria. After the peanuts have been picked, they are put into big piles like those in the picture.

Nigeria has more people than any other country in

Africa. In this big country there are 35 million people. The people belong to 250 tribes and speak 200 different languages.

In West Africa there is a little country that is like America in many ways. It is named *Liberia*. The people use American money. Boys and girls learn English in school.

This is because long ago some American Negro slaves who had become free decided to go back to Africa. White Americans helped them buy ships. The Negroes settled in West Africa and named their new country Liberia. This means Land of the Free.

The school in the picture was built by an American

Firestone

company. This company has planted many rubber trees in Liberia.

The Story of Dr. Livingstone

Many white men went to Africa to find ivory or to capture slaves. There were also men who wanted to help the Africans.

Dr. David Livingstone was a young Scotsman, a doctor, who wanted to be a missionary. He went to Africa in 1841 to help the many Africans who were sick.

Dr. Livingstone visited many parts of Africa never seen by Europeans before. He found new rivers and lakes and waterfalls. Sometimes he was attacked by African tribespeople. Once he was almost killed by a wounded lion.

Author

40

Albert Schweitzer

Dr. Livingstone died long ago while exploring Africa. But there is another famous doctor who is still living in Africa.

Dr. Albert Schweitzer is one of the most famous men in the world. He is a great musician, and he has written many books. Dr. Schweitzer could be a rich man if he wished.

Many years ago Dr. Schweitzer went to West Africa. He wanted to spend his life helping Africans. Dr. Schweitzer has built a hospital in the jungle at Lambaréné. Every day he gives medicine to sick people. Because of his work, thousands of Africans have been cured of sickness.

Troubles in Africa

The boys and girls in the picture are happy. They live in nice houses and have a place to play. In some countries, Europeans have helped Africans have better homes.

But many boys and girls do not have nice homes. Many cannot go to school because there are not enough schools or teachers.

Many Africans do not like living in colonies. They are not happy because they are ruled by white men. They want better houses and more schools.

Africans do not like it because so much land is owned.

by white farmers. Here is a picture of a European farmer who owns a big coffee plantation. In some African colonies one white farmer may own as much as 100,000 acres.

Africans want the rich farmland owned by European farmers. They say that when the European explorers came to Africa long ago they took all the best land.

Sometimes Africans and white Europeans fight one another. The big country called the Congo belonged to Belgium for many years. Even after the Congo became a free country, there was trouble between Africans and Belgians who still lived there.

Info Kenya

African soldiers killed Belgian soldiers. And Africans burned the houses belonging to the Belgians. There was fighting between different tribes too.

There has been fighting between Africans and Europeans in other parts of Africa. The people who live in colonies want to be free. Remember that our country belonged to England long ago. Americans fought against the soldiers of the King of England.

You can see a picture of United Nations soldiers who were sent to the Congo to stop the fighting.

Things to Remember about Africa

Africa is a big continent with forty different countries.

44

Some of the countries are colonies. There is trouble in Africa because the people living in colonies want to be free.

In Africa there are jungles and deserts, snow-covered mountains and lakes and rivers. Many wild animals live in Africa. There are lions and elephants, rhinos and hippos, monkeys and gorillas. There are crocodiles in the rivers and lakes.

Americans sometimes visit Africa to hunt animals or to see the beautiful mountains and lakes and rivers.

This is a picture of Murchison Falls on the Nile River.

Info Uganda

Many Africans are very poor and live in small houses. Boys and girls often cannot go to school, and many people are sick. Sometimes people are sick because they do not have good food. They do not have enough doctors and medicine.

Because of slavery long ago, many Africans were taken to our country. After the Civil War, all the slaves became free.

Our country is helping the people of Africa. American missionaries build schools and hospitals and churches. Our government sends men to Africa to teach people how to grow more food. American doctors are teaching Africans about good health.

There is rich land in Africa where good crops grow. Much of the copper we use comes from African mines. Cocoa for our chocolate and coconut oil for soap come from Africa.

This Page Is for Your Teacher

The vocabulary used in this book has been carefully selected, using as far as possible only words appearing in Dolch's list of the 2,000 commonest words for spelling. The authors have tried to develop certain important concepts as simply as possible. It is difficult, for instance, to make understandable the meaning of colonies and colonialism. As we have learned from happenings in the Congo, the effort of Africans to become free and independent can affect the United States.

SOME FACTS ABOUT AFRICA

The area of Africa is 11,500,000 square miles compared to North America's 9,300,000 square miles. The climate of Africa varies greatly. In the desert regions it is hot and dry, but temperatures may take a big drop at night. In the low-lying coastal areas it is very hot and wet. Most of the middle of the continent is a plateau rising into scattered mountains, and the climate is temperate.

While most Africans are illiterate, poor, disease-ridden, and superstitious, there are highly educated Africans. And while most people live in jungle villages, beautiful and modern cities exist. Except during the rainy season, it is possible to travel through most of the continent by automobile.

SOME AFRICAN COUNTRIES

Liberia is an independent nation, founded by freed American slaves. It has an area of 43,000 square miles and a population of 1,300,000.

Ghana, formerly called the Gold Coast, is now independent. It has an area of 91,843 square miles and almost 5,000,000 people.

Nigeria became a free member of the British Commonwealth in 1960 and has 35,000,000 people in an area of 372,647 square miles.

All of the areas once parts of French West and French Equatorial Africa are now independent nations.

The Congo, with a population of 16,000,000 and an area of 925,000 square miles, became independent of Belgium in 1960.